inspired

carpets

wise publications
london/new york/sydney

exclusive distributors:
music sales limited
8/9 frith street
london w1v 5tz
england.

music sales pty limited
120 rothschild avenue
rosebery
nsw 2018
australia

this book © copyright 1990 by
wise publications
order no. am80367
isbn 0.7119. 2347.7

music arranged by roger day
music processed by musicprint

music sales' complete catalogue lists thousands of titles and
is free from your local music shop or direct from music sales limited.
please send £1 in stamps for postage to:
music sales limited
8/9 frith street
london w1v 5tz.

printed in the united kingdom by
j.b. offset printers (marks tey) limited, marks tey, essex.

real thing

words & music by
martyn walsh, thomas hingley, craig gill,
clint boon & graham lambert.

(on %. Instr.)

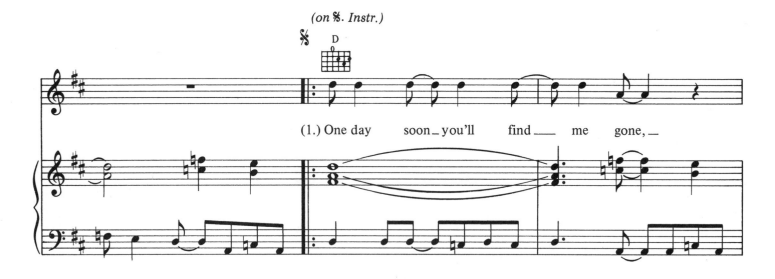

(1.) One day soon you'll find me gone,

I've no i - dea of where I am, search and search with no

VERSE 2:
Then you'll find me laughing
At what you said behind their backs
I find the truth about it funny
I find it so hard to take.

VERSE 3:
We play these games too often
We play at strangers in the bed
You search for something different
Put the gun right to my head.

song for a family

**words & music by
martyn walsh, thomas hingley, craig gill,
clint boon & graham lambert.**

rose col-oured wea-thered skin is glow-ing and the do-mi-no is at his fin-ger-

tips. And he prays each night that his fami-ly's all right and he's got

work.

1.

(2.) See the

2.

Strange as it may seem

we all pray for sim-ple things, stran-gers share your dreams, who knows what the prayers will bring?

Love and health _ is all till you fal-ter in your steps and fall we all live on dreams.

Slower

D.C. al Coda
To Coda ⊕

⊕ CODA

VERSE 2:
See the lollipop lady by the roadside
Some days the kids are so hard to control
But they bring her lots of presents on her birthday
And their little faces make her feel so old
And she prays each night her family's alright and she's got work.

VERSE 3:
See the lad on the Saturday terraces
With his collar pulled up around his chin
His side are two goals down and playing lousy
But he still believes his team is going to win
And he prays each night that his family's alright and he's got work.

this is how it feels

words & music by
martyn walsh, thomas hingley, craig gill,
clint boon & graham lambert.

(1.) Hus-band don't know what he's done, kids don't know what's wrong with mum she can't say, they can't see, put-ting it down to an-

VERSE 2:
There's a funeral in the town
Some guy from the top estate
Seems they found him under a train
And yet he had it all on a plate.

VERSE 3:
Husband don't know what he's done
Kids don't know what's wrong with mum
She can't say, they can't see
Putting it down to another bad day.

directing traffik

words & music by
martyn walsh, thomas hingley, craig gill,
clint boon & graham lambert.

read it in a book at school, ___ I read it with Jan-et and John, ___ no

13

matter how you know the man, ___ you can't trust what he's on. ___

Some-time la - ter when he's on his own, ___ what

once was mus -cle is ___ now bone.

CHORUS

I see a skull on a stick, ___ I see a ske - le - ton with

VERSE 2:
You can't judge a man by his skin
Or a book by the cover it's in
But I can't help feel it's true
The devil's got a hand in you
In a world of laughter where the madmen thrive
You're sewing up your death shroud from the inside.

VERSE 3:
I read it in a book at school
I read it with Janet and John
No matter how you know the man
You can't trust what he's on
In a world of laughter where the madmen thrive
You're sewing up your death shroud from the inside.

besides me

words & music by
martyn walsh, thomas hingley, craig gill,
clint boon & graham lambert.

I'm ____ too tired ____ to lis - ten to an - y - thing ____

me.

VERSE 2:
I don't want to watch you
All the stupid things you say
All the times add up to nothing
Everything you do or say
Too much, it always costs too much
It always costs too much
It always costs too much.

VERSE 3:
I won't ask you questions
Time will pass you by
Left alone in this world
You are the strangest one
Too much, you always say too much
You always say too much
You always say too much.

many happy returns

words & music by
martyn walsh, thomas hingley, craig gill,
clint boon & graham lambert.

VERSE 2:
I try to get away
But all of the time you follow
It's just a moth to a flame
It's getting too hard to live here
It's getting too hard to see you
This is what you have done to me.

memories of you

**words & music by
martyn walsh, thomas hingley, craig gill,
clint boon & graham lambert.**

she comes in the fall

words & music by
martyn walsh, thomas hingley, craig gill,
clint boon & graham lambert.

in the short time that I have ___ got to
know you I have found here a
wrong way ___ to go a-bout it it's just
this fear, the fear I have ___ to go a-bout it.

(3° Vocal)

You should learn to walk, — you should learn to walk — be-fore you crawl.

You should learn to walk, — you should learn to walk — be-fore you crawl.

You should learn to walk, — you should learn to walk — be-fore you crawl.

You should learn to walk, — you should learn to walk — be-fore you crawl. Here she

VERSE 2:
Back she returns there, he's always sat in the same chair
All you feel is, the harder edge and the heat
I have found here, a wrong way to go about it
It's just this fear, the fear I have to go about you.

monkey on my back

**words & music by
martyn walsh, thomas hingley, craig gill,
clint boon & graham lambert.**

So here we are up in your room __ and

I can feel the dan - ger __ and you tell me

it will be soon ___ so I con - trol my an - ger. ___

But you say there's no dan - ger _____ that's when I can see ___

___ your fear. ___ The

mon - key
There's a mon - key on my back ___ on my back

There's a mon - key

VERSE 2:
I try to tell you how I feel
It's just me counting the hours
It's not so unreal
And you've got no special powers
But when I see the morning light
Don't tell me it ain't right.

sun don't shine

words & music by
martyn walsh, thomas hingley, craig gill,
clint boon & graham lambert.

(1.) You wrote you love me, ___

well that's _ fine but now_ you're gone and _ the

sun it ___ don't _ shine. One thing's_ for

cer - tain, ___ it was ___ good ___ fun.

But now_ you're gone there is ___ no ___ sun.

VERSE 2:
The first kiss, in your arms
You were the victim of nobody's charms
We had something good we can't take away
Will you see me tomorrow, well who can say.

VERSE 3:
I speak in words that you can understand
So why should it be that you won't hold my hand
You burnt me, just like a fire
There's no love and here there's no desire.

inside my head

words & music by
martyn walsh, thomas hingley, craig gill,
clint boon & graham lambert.

burnt.

[Continue RIFF 2°]

We're gon-na be to-geth-er ve-ry soon,—

I won't be danc-ing by the light of the moon.— Don't tell me you don't

D.S. al Fine

care   for   me ___   that   ain't the way   it   was   meant   to

be.

VERSE 2:
She speaks a language
I've never heard
Keep me guessing
With every word.

VERSE 3:
She shows me things
I've never seen
Takes me places
I've never been.

move

**words & music by
martyn walsh, thomas hingley, craig gill,
clint boon & graham lambert.**

To Coda ⊕

42

VERSE 2:
Layers of skin, I've been touched within
Heard it in your voice, read it in your eyes
Right down the line, you can't take the truth
My head is sore, I can't feel you move.

sackville

words & music by
martyn walsh, thomas hingley, craig gill,
clint boon & graham lambert.

(1.) You once had a home and job___ a fa - mi - ly___ and pride ___ but we all have a price we'll

keep a warm __ fire burn - ing in your soul.

'Cause you're gon-na spend a black night, con - sole a

sad man, in a hun - gry ci - ty with a

mil - lion hun - gry hearts. ___

When you stand in Sack - ville
it's a diffe-rent world from the one ___ you ___ knew ___ where lit - tle
boys meet lit - tle girls. ___ ___ it's a cold and trem-bling girl ___
___ leans in - to a strange ___ car, ___ nods un -

spo - ken words to ___ an un - seen dri - ver sit - ting there. ___

Instr. rpt. ad lib.

Ad lib. to Fade

VERSE 2:

As you tread your path, through a jaundiced corridor
Where each day has no beginning and no end
There are those out here, who claim to be so good
I suspect that Jesus holidayed in hell
Oh what you'd do for a hot drink, or a warm coat
What you'd give for a means to get you outta here
It rains upon your head, lines on your face become
Rivers into which you cry your secret tears.

VERSE 3:

The first night we saw you we were laughing at you
We were hanging out the side of the Cortina
Oh yeah you seemed so strong stronger than a man could ever be
Laughing with your sisters in the rain
Dancing on a kerbstone when last you saw her
But when the trick goes wrong there's no one there to help her
There's not a thing that I can do about it
I guess I'll just go home and write a song about it.

Chorus